Top 10 Mistakes You Can't Afford to Make When Starting a New Business

by **Mia Haley**

Top 10 Mistakes You Can't Afford to Make When Starting a MaNew Business

DISCLAIMER

DEDICATION

This book is dedicated to my mother, Lorraine Lee, who has always been my biggest "Fan". You have supported my dreams and goals before I even understood the meaning of support. You've been supportive through all of the successes as well as the failures, and that support has been so important to have. Thank you. There are no words for the Love and Appreciation I have for you.

And, thanks to my husband, Carl and son, Jordan for all your love and patience.

Contents

CHAPTER 1

Introduction

Much of the information provided in this book is based on my own personal experience as an entrepreneur / small business owner and it includes real-life "lessons learned." I am writing this book, because I feel as though we went into the most expensive business venture thus far, without all the rules to the game, and I want to share the top 10 basic rules with you. The object of the game of business is to *"win"*, but sometimes we start playing the game before we read all of the instructions and understand all of the rules.

This short book contains basic rules to the game of entrepreneurship and starting a small business. It encourages you to pursue your dreams of entrepreneurship, but it also alerts you to the dangers of not conducting the proper research. The information within is directed to the aspiring or new entrepreneur who is trying to work his or her way through the starting process. Please realize that much more research on business ownership will be required on your part, but this book will give you a good start or additional help. For the purpose of this book, I will be talking solely about starting a small business.

A small business is defined as an independent business having fewer than 500 employees. Small businesses are so important because they have generated 65% of the net new jobs over the past 17 years and they pay 44% of the total U.S. private payroll, according to the U.S. Dept. of Commerce, Census Bureau and Intl. Trade Admin. This source also indicates that, in 2009, there were 27.5 million businesses in the United States, with 52% being home based businesses and 2% being franchises.

This book contains my small business journey as a case study for you. It serves as one of many examples.

My husband has been my business partner and a part of my entrepreneur journey since I met him, in 1992, and is still a great source of encouragement today. You will notice that I mention his role often, when I mention the word *"we"*. If you are married, or have a significant other, the support they provide can be a key element to an aspiring entrepreneur.

In the book, "The Millionaire Mind", by Thomas J. Stanley, Ph.D., 2001, p. 238 & 239, it states:

> "Couples who share common interests tend to remain married, and there is a correlation between length of marriage and net worth. Having a common interest in wealth-building activities is key for couples who wish to become financially independent, and the most common of these activities is owning and operating a family business."

Stanley also wrote the book, "The Millionaire Next Door." Both books are excellent reads for an aspiring entrepreneur or persons looking to build wealth.

I'm definitely not claiming that all of our business ventures have been successful and, in actuality, many were not, but they've all been great learning experiences that have eventually led to personal successes. I believe that mistakes are the steps toward wisdom, and setbacks do not mean our dreams are unattainable. I'm not claiming to be the "expert" with all the answers, but I do believe that I have gained knowledge, both from my personal business experiences and the experiences of others, that can benefit the aspiring or new entrepreneur. I believe that I'm able to give my experience and viewpoint in a way that many "know-it-all experts" will gloss over or present in a way that is too complicated for the aspiring or new entrepreneur.

In this particular book, I call myself a subject matter expert on the topic of *"Mistakes NOT to Make when Starting a New Small Business"*. It is advice on what not to do, in order to help your decisions on what you should do. I've made many business mistakes, but I hope that sharing my top 10 will save YOU valuable money and time, by helping you to avoid common pitfalls, therefore helping to make decisions that will lead to business success. I'll be challenging you to take a hard look at your ideas and preparedness. You will be applying the concept of learning from the mistakes of others, as well as learning from your own mistakes. But, keep in mind that reading this book will not stop you from making all mistakes, as that is not my intent. I am here only to help you overcome some of the biggest, most common mistakes new business owners make.

Starting a new business venture is both exciting and risky. In the beginning, I started like most dreamers, wanting to be my own boss, with the starry-eyed dream of business ownership, the *"American Dream"*. What I soon realized is that sometimes it can lead to a *"nightmare"*. My first business ventures included network marketing, creating products to sell on eBay, a staffing service (computer consulting), being a real estate agent, photography, trading stocks as a day trader and my most expensive learning experience, owning a franchise restaurant. Our lessons learned as restaurant owners were the lessons that stood out the most, because of the high investment COST (Yikes!). I've gained a wealth of knowledge and lessons learned from all of my business experiences, but in this particular book, many of my examples will come from the restaurant business experience.

Although many of the "Top 10 Lessons Learned" shared in this book are based on our restaurant business experience and research, the concepts can be used for almost any start-up business. As you read, don't let the challenges discourage you. Keep in mind that the only people who never fail are those who never try, so don't worry about the judgments of others who are afraid to try but want to judge you.

My husband and I owned and operated a fast food franchise restaurant from 2004 – 2007, for 4 years. This was our most expensive entrepreneur project, where we received *baptism by fire* from the school of *hard knocks*. It's a tough school. Our corporate work backgrounds are in computer engineering and telecommunications. We were very successful in our corporate careers, but we were on a mission to become our own boss. We decided on a hot wings franchise restaurant that looked exciting and what we thought fit within our budget. The idea was stuck in our heads that the best business models operated in brick and mortar, or physical buildings, and we wanted our own business located in a physical building so bad we could taste it.

In our restaurant, we served 16 flavors of hot wings with veggie sticks, french fries, chicken tenders, fried fish, coleslaw, salads, desserts, and lots of side items. Our foods were cooked per the customer's order; we offered table seating with sports on big screen TVs and had a sports theme for the decor. It was a franchise that seemed to be a simple concept.

We quickly discovered, however, that just because it is a franchise concept, does not necessarily mean it will be successful. As a matter of fact, we felt that, although this was a franchise restaurant, it ended up feeling more like a "mom and pop" business because of the lack of brand awareness and corporate support, and the small number of other local locations (this is hindsight analysis, of course).

Don't get me wrong, I'm not going to blame others for our mistakes — and you'll see I make this point clear in later chapters. We made plenty of mistakes but, looking back now on the experience and understanding those things we didn't know to look for in a franchise, we could have avoided many pitfalls by following some basic rules. At the end of the day, the reasons this business did not work falls squarely on our shoulders. We lacked the industry experience, didn't plan well enough and didn't have enough cash flow.

Here's the bonus lesson I learned: "Ultimately, the cause of a business failure is based on the owners' abilities, character, education and capacity." For example, we thought our smarts, abilities and success in corporate engineering would automatically transfer to the restaurant business (WRONG!).

This is one of the types of books that I wish I had read before venturing into the restaurant business. You'll need to do your research on small business, do your due diligence in your industry and understand your market and marketing. Read many books on your subject and the subject of business ownership. I'm hoping you'll find helpful information in this book as you move forward in your entrepreneurial journey.

CHAPTER 2

Get to know yourself

Many people overlook this important step in the beginning of their entrepreneurial journey and end up losing valuable time in a business or career that doesn't match who they really are. Most of the time, we find that looking for our niche or true talent is a process of trial and error. Few know exactly what their purpose is and exactly what they are supposed to be doing early in life, myself included.

The trial and error process can be very costly and time consuming if you don't start with this step. I believe this is one of the most important "lessons learned" because it starts the course of all your actions. It's so important, because if you don't take the time to find out what you truly love to do, you will not be as dedicated to riding out the rough times, which could lead to failure. I didn't start here in my entrepreneurial quest—and I wish that I had.

Getting to know yourself involves questioning yourself and searching for the true answers. The concept and questions below aren't new, but most people still won't take the time to do these exercises that help give them direction. I truly believe that if I had taken the time to ask myself the following questions and had answered them truthfully, I would not have chosen the restaurant business model in which I lost a lot of money and time. Later, as I looked back on this particular experience, I realized the business model I chose did not fit who I am and where my interests really lie.

The restaurant business might be just the right match for you, but completing this important process will help confirm your decision. I believe you should find out what you're good at, stick with it and work at becoming really great at it. The best investment you can make is in yourself.

In the end, all was not lost; I did take those lemons and, eventually, made lemonade. I took the time to learn more about myself and about business. I've taken my experiences, knowledge, research and those hard lessons learned, and I am now using them to benefit others — in turn, benefiting myself.

Through these experiences and chain of events, I've discovered what I truly enjoy and what I'm good at: researching, reading, writing, coaching, consulting and teaching. I love it! I've found a need in the marketplace that matches the skills I enjoy using most. I perform these tasks all day long, as an entrepreneur, and it doesn't feel like work.

Ask yourself the following questions and give them some serious thought. You may even want to discuss this with someone close who you trust. I've also learned that finding an accountability partner is a huge benefit in life (start looking for one or two). We need constant inspiration and, sometimes, others see strengths and weaknesses in us that we don't see in ourselves and can help us stay true to who we really are. The key to finding an accountability partner is finding someone you trust, who will be honest and give you constructive critique. A bonus would be if they had the same business interests as you.

Here's the part people hate to do, but is necessary. Find a piece of paper and write the answers to the following questions (yes, you need to write them down; trust me, it works). Be sure to give yourself plenty of time to think of the true answers, even if you need to come back and answer the questions later. Your answers will be very different from mine, but I'll give you a short version of my answers to help get your creative juices flowing.

1. **Question**: What experiences in your life have had the most influence on you? **Answer**: For me, it has been the ownership and responsibilities of the restaurant business and the many lessons learned. Through my experience and journey with many ventures, I've finally found my career passion. My life also changed when I started reading many non-fiction books and learning about others' successes and failures. The more you learn, the more you'll earn. On a personal level, my life experience as a mother has had the most positive influence of all.

2. **Question**: What do you think are your natural skills, talents and fascinations? **Answer**: I believe a few of my natural talents are researching, reading, writing, listening, coaching, teaching, inspiring others and storytelling. I'm also fascinated with learning the history of business, economics, investing and wealth building.

3. **Question**: Make a list of all your skills (no matter how irrelevant some may seem) and then list what kinds of people and environments might benefit from those skills. **Answer**: Researching, reading and writing — gave me the clue that I would enjoy being a writer, writing as a blogger and author of books. I wish I would have taken this clue seriously long ago. Listening skills — many people tell me that I'm a good listener, which means that I hear and see things that others miss. I connect well with people in one on one settings — this is useful in independent consulting environments such as counseling (I was once a career counselor) or in coaching small groups. Teaching, storytelling and inspiring others — this is useful in many ways, including being a writer, public speaking events and teaching niche subjects to small groups. I am detail oriented and have very good planning and organization skills — these skills served well in my career as a telecommunications planner and engineer. Of course, there are many more environments in which these skills would be useful, but these are just a few examples.

4. **Question**: What education or professional backgrounds can you draw from? **Answer:** I have a Bachelor's degree in Communications and Public Relations, with a minor in English. I've learned a lot from reading many self-help and non-fiction books on how to succeed in life, business and wealth building. I have over 16 years of corporate environment experience including telecommunications, as an

outside plant engineer, real estate and insurance sales, career counseling, customer service environments and many types of entrepreneurial ventures including sales, internet marketing, franchise owner, writer and author of books.

5. **Question:** What instincts have you followed that have paid off for you in the past? **Answer:** My instincts to take different entrepreneurial risks and not be afraid to fail, not listening to negative talk and constantly pursuing my dreams and purpose have all paid off for me. Sometimes, you may have to try many different opportunities before you discover the right fit, but the only way you will discover this is to get over your fear of failure and try anyway. Not confronting your fears will keep you from growing and most entrepreneurs are all about learning and growing.

6. **Can you start to see where this exercise is going and what you are learning about yourself? If you need help getting started, try talking with your newly found accountability partner I mentioned above.**

7. **Question:** Which personal relationships, professional connections and social networks are you a part of and which do you enjoy most? **Answer:** To be honest, not as many as I should be a part of – and this is a work in progress for me. I do participate in a few professional, special interest groups such as www.smartpassiveincome.com, which is related to my internet marketing business, an authors' special interest group, related to writing books and real estate

investment clubs, to learn more about real estate investing. My social networks include the people I meet at church, people I meet while learning ballroom dancing, other parents I meet who are involved with their kids' activities and, of course, family and friends. I am looking to join a few *mastermind* groups also.

8. **Question:** In what environments do you feel most alive, energized or at ease? **Answer:** Small groups, special interests groups related to finance/budgeting, investing, business, real estate, writing books, etc. Environments that allow me to be flexible and use creative thinking. Environments that encourage growth, learning, self-help and positive thinking all keep me inspired and pumped! I also try to be around positive people who prefer these same types of environments.

9. **Question:** What current moments in your life bring you the most satisfaction? **Answer:** When I'm strengthening my spiritual connection, special moments with my son, my husband, mom and other family members, attending workshops where I'm learning and inspired to move forward with my dreams, when I pursue a goal and reach it (and I have many).

10. **Question:** What qualifies as "fun" for you, even if it feels like work to others? **Answer:** Reading, writing, researching my special interest topics, learning more about business and investing, teaching and inspiring others, etc.

In addition to answering the questions above, here's the second part of the exercise. I know it may sound boring and unexciting, but it's the small, simple tasks that help build solid foundations. I wish I had taken the time to take these steps before deciding on a business model and spending thousands of dollars.

On the back of your paper, write down "my loves" on one side and "my hates" on the other. For example, my personal list looks a little like this:

My loves:

1. Travel and spending time with family

2. Reading, researching, writing and learning new things

3. Storytelling, through words and pictures

4. Decorating my home and spending time at home

5. Socializing with friends and family

6. Photography and Videography

7. Inspiring and coaching others to make their dreams or visions attainable

8. Having quiet time to meditate

My hates:

1. Being in confined places

2. Being micromanaged and micromanaging others

3. Not being paid my worth

4. Feeling like I'm wasting time

5. Not having the money or flexible time to shop or travel as I want to

6. Not knowing if my future is secure

7. Repetitious work and becoming bored

This is also called the *WHY* list, which means this is *WHY* you will make sacrifices and work hard trying to do the things you love to do. The *WHY* list is very important and will help you stay committed to goals when things get difficult, and they WILL get difficult. There will be days when you ask yourself *WHY* am I dealing with these issues and tasks that I really don't feel like dealing with? Is it worth it? You'll return to this sheet of paper periodically and remember your *WHY*. It will remind you of the big picture of *WHY* you work so hard — to be able to do more of the things you love and less of the things you hate. You'll get re-energized and re-focused in order to reach your goals.

BONUS: In keeping with your *WHY* list, if you wanted to become even more detailed and expand on the above exercise, you can do the following exercise also. On the bottom of that same piece of paper, identify what you *don't want*, and then identify what you *do want*. My list looks a little like this:

I Don't want to:

1. Work an 8-5 or a strict schedule

2. Be stuck in a cubicle

3. Feel like I'm babysitting other adults to do their work

4. Not be fully compensated for the work I do

5. Be limited on taking long vacations

6. Ask permission to take personal time off

7. Feel like my work isn't making a difference

8. Be bored or feel like I'm wasting time

9. Worry about paying bills or if I will have a nice retirement

I <u>Do</u> want to:

1. Have a flexible schedule

2. Make money while I sleep, with passive income

3. Be my own boss where I'm always learning something new

4. Spend lots of time with family and friends

5. Travel and be able to work at the same time

6. Shop when I want to

7. Be able to help my family financially

8. Have more time to explore my purpose in life

9. Work through my bucket list of fun things I've never done

Now here's the icing on the cake and the last part of the exercise! This one should be fun. Again, this is not a new concept, or activity, when working in the "self- help" arena, but it is a process that most people will skip. Visualize what your *Perfect Work Day* would look like if there were no limitations on what it could be. Write a short paragraph describing what your ideal workday would look like from the time you wake up in the morning, until you go to bed that evening. **Then we're going to see if your *loves*, *likes* and *perfect work day* fit into your *business model* idea.** A sample of my ideal work day looks something like this:

First of all, since I like to travel, I would like the flexibility of being able to conduct my work from anywhere in the world. So that means that I could work remotely on the computer. I would wake up around 8ish in the morning, because I'm not a morning person. I would have about 45 minutes of meditation and then I would work about 3 hours a day (check out the book "The 4-Hour Workweek" by Timothy Ferriss—it's an excellent entrepreneurs' source). I would have breakfast with my family and a little playtime with my son before he goes to school. As I sit on the beach, I'd spend about an hour or so reading a book, article or magazine related to my business industry. I'd work on my laptop for a couple of hours, maybe make a few business phone calls, and then I'd be off to meet friends for lunch or an adventure. My business would not require me to physically be working at any particular location or time. The business would be mostly automated and would make money whether I work that day or not. After lunch, I would do a little shopping, possibly meet with a special interest group to network, and then I'd be back home for dinner, to spend time with my son, to help with homework and enjoy quality time with husband. My days could easily change with new adventures because I would be able to work remotely and most of my businesses would be on autopilot. This is the type of ideal work-days I am pursuing.

Wasn't that FUN? Does it sound like a fairytale dream? I thought so too, until I met people who are living their dream! If they can, why can't I? Well, let me tell you, this "perfect day" did not fit anywhere close to the restaurant business model I chose. As a matter of fact, the restaurant business model fit hardly any of my *loves* or fascinations, professional background or fun work environments. Your first thought may be, "Yes, but how realistic is my above described work day?" After doing my research, I found that it's actually very realistic for many people. There are business models that fit my perfect work-day and people who are enjoying this type of work everyday. I had to first let my mind go there, then research and list the steps I needed to take in order to make it happen. This is the process I'm asking you to do.

First, you must be honest with who you are and what you really want. I do believe that you'll need both passion and knowledge in order to make a real difference in life. You must first figure out what your passions are and what motivates you. Then you need to use your knowledge, research and experience to figure out how to take the necessary steps to make it happen.

Your passion will keep you motivated; acquiring knowledge will keep you from making every mistake under the sun and wasting too much time. Passion without knowledge is dangerous and can be reckless, but knowledge without passion is sad because you have nothing to drive you forward or to motivate you. Finding your passion is like finding your *WHY* and that's half the battle. That's why this step in the process is so important.

CHAPTER 3

Pay off your personal debt before you start a business

It's simple, right? Pay off all your personal debt before you start a business to increase your chances of success. This lesson learned is major and, since I've made this mistake and have researched and learned about Dave Ramsey, the get-out-of-debt guru, it all seems crystal clear now. For further research on this lesson, I recommend reading "The Total Money Makeover" by Dave Ramsey. Back when we started as entrepreneurs, if you would have said this to us in one sentence, it would have gone in one ear and come out the other. Our excuse would have been, "That's crazy, we need that cash money to start a business," and "this will delay our dream." But, if we had read Ramsey's book completely, I believe our response would have been different. This is why reading non-fiction books and acquiring the knowledge they provide is so important.

We had all kinds of excuses for why we should not do this step first. For example, here's what we did: paid off a few credit cards before we started this business, but still carried two school loans, two car notes, a couple of credit cards and a mortgage. When the business began to struggle, it <u>could</u> support itself, but it <u>could not</u> support us. It could not provide my husband a salary to replace his existing income.

Again, I wish we had taken the time to pay off all of our personal debt before we committed so much money into the restaurant business. You have an opportunity to do this process the right way, so hear me out.

Let me give you the basic reasons why carrying personal debt and starting a new business venture with a major amount of money invested does not work. What we did not budget for was the learning curve and costly mistakes. In the beginning, we used about $150K of our own personal savings and received $150K in an SBA loan. We were so happy and proud that we were approved for an SBA loan. We felt confident in our research and business plan, since it was accepted by several banks which were willing to invest money in our plan. We shopped our loan and submitted our business plan and application to several banks. The banks interviewed us, reviewed our plan—including the pro-forma—estimated financial figures and application (personal assets). There were two banks that approved our application. Although we thought, and so did the bank, that there was sufficient research and supporting documents, we were still missing vital information and were under funded.

Our plan was to have my husband work full time in the restaurant. I would continue working my corporate engineering job full time and work at the restaurant part time, on the weekends. My husband would receive a salary from the business's profits until the business could afford for me to join him full time. We figured my corporate income added to his salary from the business would be enough to pay our personal expenses, with the additional business profits invested back into the business for growth.

Have you ever heard the saying, "Anything that can go wrong will go wrong", also known as Murphy's Law? So, how do you plan for that? Keep reading and you'll find out.

Much of our starter money was used for the new construction build-out in the shopping center's building, where we leased a space. This was a newly constructed building, and the landlord offered about $20K toward the construction build out for each tenant space, and basically gave us an empty shell to build the inside of our restaurant.

We were responsible for adding the plumbing, concrete, electrics, AC, heating and drywall. The construction build-out of our location ended up costing at least double the $50K estimated. Our estimates were based on what we were told by the corporate franchise and other franchise owners. They were wrong; this was a major hit in our pocket. We didn't get actual bids from project managers and contractors until after we had spent $20K for the initial franchise fee and paid $4K for the architecture blueprints needed for construction. Basically we had already spent $24K upfront without conducting the proper research.

With construction, there can be many unexpected events in the beginning, or throughout the construction work, that could cost extra money you don't anticipate. Even though these unexpected issues decreased our start up cash flow — that was needed for the opening of our business — we worked through the issues and continued pushing forward. One way we ended up saving money was to have my husband become the on-site project manager and negotiate discounts with many of the contractors himself. He had prior project management experience in the corporate environment, so we used this to work to our advantage.

Our planned opening day was delayed due to construction issues and permitting issues from the city that were out of our control. But, don't forget, even though we were not open yet, we still needed to start payments on our SBA loan (just like a house note, it must be paid every month on time), rent for leased space and our franchise fee.

On our opening day, we were so excited to serve our customers and start making money. For the first few weeks and months, sales were great! Then came the tapering off that most businesses eventually experience after the newness wears off, when the real numbers start showing up. The *real* monthly numbers were not consistently as high as we had projected, but we just thought, "Ok, we'll have to find ways to cut our operating expenses, right?"

Here's a summary of what happened. 1. Our construction estimates were more than double what we had budgeted. 2. We opened the business later than we had planned, due to the landlord delivering the leased space to us late, which meant their construction crew ended late and our construction crew started late. With each day we were delayed, we were not making money from sales. If we had conducted thorough research regarding lease negotiations, or had hired an attorney, we would have known about this type of risk and how to mitigate it. For example, we would have included in our rental lease, "To charge the landlord a fee each day they were late in delivering the leased space to us," thereby recouping some of the sales we were losing by not being open. 3. Finally, after a few months of being open, our sales numbers started to drop and stabilize. This low stabilization affected our cash flow. It was a lot less than what was needed and didn't give us any profits. We increased our marketing strategies, but the sales were still not increasing sufficiently. Also, the costs of goods were market driven, which meant they could go up or down quickly, without notice, because the corporate franchise did not have locked vendor rates, which they should have. Depending on the season and the economy, our food cost from the vendor could double what we had budgeted. Murphy was banging hard on our door.

Our monthly expenses that were fixed comprised of: SBA loan payment, rent for leased space, franchise fee percentage and city fees. Then we had the other expenses that could go up or down: utilities, employee payroll, food cost, administrative cost, marketing, equipment and repairs, etc. These are the expenses you have control over and can make cuts to, in order to save money. For example, to save on payroll expenses, my husband worked from open to close as the manager/ owner and, in the evenings and on weekends, I came in to work, so we were both working around the clock to make up for the cash flow shortage.

To save on food costs, we learned quickly how to manage food inventory. This meant we only ordered enough food for the week, in order to keep more cash in our bank rather than sitting on the shelf, also known as "just in time inventory." You need to be careful when using this method, because you don't want to get into a cycle where you are constantly sold out of a product that customers really like.

For the first couple of years, the business made enough money to sustain itself, but not enough profits were made to come close to replacing my husband's corporate salary. That meant that my engineering job provided the only income to cover our expenses at home. We could sustain on my income alone for about a year, without needing my husband to have an income from the business. Our personal living expenses had not changed, so we still needed money for mortgage, homeowners' association fees, utilities, insurances, groceries, two car notes, two school loans, credit cards and house maintenance. We ended up getting behind on our personal bills because our living expenses were more than my corporate job could sustain.

Here's the lesson learned from this chapter: if we had paid off all our consumer debt before starting this business, we would not have needed any income from the business. It would have given the business time to grow. This is one reason to become *debt free* first, before you invest a large sum of your money into a business.

In order to deal with this issue, we had the bright idea of getting an additional business loan to not only replace the *cash reserve* shortage for the business, but also so we could get caught up on personal living expenses we had gotten behind on. Do you see the downward spiral here? I know you may think something like this could never happen to you, but it can and does happen.

So, based on my experience and looking back on how our personal finances should have been managed: 1. We should have paid off all of our consumer debt first. 2. We should have had 6 months' emergency savings set aside to be used for household emergencies only. 3. We should have had a written household budget that was based on my corporate job's income only, in the event that the business was unable to provide an income in the formative years.

Yes, this was my personal experience, but don't think that this—or other unexpected events—can't happen to you. Again, it's wise to not only learn from your mistakes but also the mistakes of others.

CHAPTER 4

Use your own cash to fund a new business

Using your own cash to fund a new business does not include using your monthly household living expenses, your six-month emergency savings, or retirement savings—those should be set aside. This is a hard lesson learned, because it requires patience and sacrifice (something most of us struggle with at some point). You will need patience and sacrifice to save this money and not spend it on consumer items such as cars, credit cards, electronics, clothes, traveling, eating out, and etc. Focus and determination will play a key role in your success.

So, back to my story, we made the mistake of using our retirement savings and our six month emergency savings, and we went even further by receiving an SBA loan for the start up money. We were *all in*, finding ourselves with all of our eggs in one basket. When you feel the need to be *all in*, it is an indication that you really can't afford the business you are getting into. Of course, if we could do it over, we would not have used those funds, or the SBA loan. Our total monies needed may be more or less than what you need for your business idea, but the concept is still the same.

Here's the lesson in this chapter: we should've chosen a business concept that was within our cash budget at the time or saved more money first. It's that simple; it's worth the upfront patience and sacrifice. For a new business, it was a struggle to make the SBA loan payments when sales were not as we'd expected, and when we needed our emergency savings for household emergencies, it was not there. In hindsight analysis, this situation could have easily been avoided if we had followed a few basic rules of the game (to be exact, the top 10 rules I'm sharing with you). The financial mistakes in this chapter and the previous chapter could sink your boat quickly and set you back for years to come!

Here's an alternate way of looking at it: why not choose a business you can build slowly—using the start-up cash you've set aside and the profits when they are made—rather than choosing a business that seems as though it will grow quickly, but may have many hidden risks, whereby you could lose everything? Again, you'll need to have patience and be willing to make sacrifices—which is one of the secrets to success.

Also, completing the exercise in Chapter 2, "Getting to Know Yourself," will help give you the direction on the type of business that is most suitable to your personality. If I had completed this exercise, I believe I would have realized the restaurant business model was not a good fit for me. Even though most of my money was invested in retirement accounts and emergency savings, I still had about $25K remaining that I could have used to start and grow a small business.

Consider the following scenario: what if we had started the food business with $25K (assuming this was our passion)?

We could have begun by buying a food cart and purchasing used equipment to cater local events and participate as a food vendor in events such as parties, local fairs, outside concerts, etc. We would then use our *profits* to grow the business and expand.

Eventually, this could have led to opening the brick and mortar restaurant we operated, but by using our own money from *profits* and not from an SBA loan. This would have also allowed one of us, if not both, to continue working a regular corporate job until enough *profits* were being made.

In the beginning, while trying to grow and work through the unknown, we would not have had the overhead expenses of leasing a building, franchise fees, the SBA loan payment, as much in payroll and other overhead expenses. If the business did not work out, we would have only lost around $25,000 of our own cash, instead of around $300,000+. This was a hard and expensive lesson learned for me. Understand and consider all your options. I've learned you are not required to take the most extreme route to meet your end goal. The financial risks I take now are a lot more calculated, researched and successful.

Also, this is not to say that you should follow all the steps we should have taken in this particular case study, but this example is to challenge you to **THINK**. Look further into your plan and think of scenarios of how you can reach your goals using your own money, while keeping yourself out of debt. You can do it with just a little patience and sacrifice and, of course, lots of in-depth research. It's challenging, but doable.

CHAPTER 5

Don't cut your funding too close

I have touched on this subject a lot already in the last two chapters, so this will be short and sweet. This specific lesson learned is a big part of the 10-step program, therefore it should be highlighted. Do not cut your funding too close; you need to have <u>at least</u> 2 or 3 times the cash reserves your business plan requires. In other words, when you calculate projected monies needed for the first few years of your business, multiply it times 2 or 3, and this is closer to what you'll really need. At a minimum, it usually costs twice as much, will take twice as long and you will work twice as harder than you had planned.

There will be unexpected business and personal issues arising, there will be learning curves and there may also be slow sales. If you do not account for these situations and do not have enough cash reserves, this could be detrimental to your business. We now understand how we did not budget enough cash reserves in the beginning. When there were maintenance issues, there were months of slow sales and an increase in food costs, all arising at the same time; we were really struggling with cash flow. Eventually, our line of credit dried up and we begin borrowing money from family members and using other types of risky funding, which leads you deeper into debt.

As I mentioned in the previous chapters, we created a financial spreadsheet on what we projected our start up expenses would include. We included items such as construction costs, SBA loan payments, franchise fees, rent, marketing, utilities, city fees, payroll, cost of food, administrative costs and repair costs. We based a few of these start-up costs on projections we received from the corporate franchise, those of other franchise owners and industry market research of our own.

Our projected customer sales were based on input from the corporate franchise and our market research, including who our customers were going to be (in the area), how much they eat out, how much our average sales ticket would be and the estimated customer traffic flow in the shopping center. Some of our research came from the Chamber of Commerce and the city public records. We also conducted a head-count analysis based on how many customers visited the other franchises and projected sales of each customer food ticket.

Lesson learned: give yourself a fighting chance; at least double or triple your cash flow estimate.

CHAPTER 6

Research the financial reports first

Research, Research, Research, and then have a couple of business owners who are experienced in that business model to evaluate and review your research with you.

Whether you are buying a franchise or an independently owned business, be sure to see the actual financial reports, as a part of your research. If the prospective seller doesn't want to share this vital information with you, turn and run fast. If the company is not transparent, this is an indication that valuable information is being hidden or left out, information that could mean your success or failure.

If you were buying stock from a public company, you would get a prospectus to analyze the financial data which includes risk information. Why would you not do the same for a business you are buying? I don't mean just the numbers or prospectus for the *franchise* or a *corporate office*, but specific monthly/annual reports you can analyze from individual locations that are in operation (no problem if you have to sign a non-disclosure agreement).

We learned this lesson the hard way with our restaurant. Our franchise was not a public company on Wall Street, so the prospectus (financial) information was limited. A private company does not have to share certain information with the public, such as detailed financials and risk factors.

Secondly, the franchise gave a general broad view of typical store expenses and sales numbers. They gave us a data sheet with a range of typical expenses, including the construction build-out. Finally, the company directed us to the owners of individual store locations, if we wanted more detail about financial numbers. The individual store owners did not want to share their actual financial reports. They reviewed our proposed forecast of projected sales and expenses and gave us feedback. This should have been a red flashing light signal to us that trouble was ahead.

Based on the general expenses and sales information we received from the corporate franchise, a few individual franchise owners and our research, we created our own financial spreadsheet of expected sales and expenses. We then had the corporate office and the individual franchise owners review it and give us feedback. We figured that if our numbers were off, they would be the ones who could help correct them. Once they confirmed that our numbers looked accurate, we felt good about our start. We even convinced the loan officer at the bank (SBA loan) that our numbers were accurate.

But, in actuality, we should've easily doubled or tripled the cash flow monies needed for our start-up estimates. We didn't include enough cash reserve for the unexpected — the natural learning curve, errors or delays in our budget. Eventually the business started making a small profit, and we learned how to manage expenses better, but, by then, we were already too far in the negative on personal expenses, which affected our business. There wasn't enough cash flow from the beginning. There were major issues that were not anticipated and were not included in our expense budget, which are common mistakes for new start up business.

To give you another example, shortly after we opened there were plumbing problems in our building with the grease trap. Grease traps are plumbing devices restaurants need, designed to intercept most greases and solids before they enter a water disposal system. We assumed the building owners would handle this problem and expense. After all, it was city requirement for the building, it was the landlord's building and we were the tenants. But this was not the case; the owners of the building let us know this was a problem and expense we were responsible for. We checked our lease agreement and, sure enough, they were right. We didn't have an attorney review the lease for us in detail (more on this in chapter 8).

This is an indication that the research we thought we conducted was not detailed enough. You may never get ALL of the detailed information needed or the correct information, but there is a certain level of basic information that should be collected or steps that should be taken when starting a new business. Your job is to do the detailed research, find out those basic steps and follow the process correctly. When you do not, it could lead to very costly mistakes and the risk of failure is higher.

CHAPTER 7

Know the business you are in

Work in someone else's business before you commit. This exercise gives you a personal look at what you're getting into and a chance to see "best practices," which means that you have an upfront look at a few business practices to learn what works and what doesn't work.

After looking back on our experience, we wish we had worked for an owner (part-time) in the type of restaurant we operated. Working within a business first could give you a real sense of the business workflow and the opportunity to see if you would really like to do a certain type of work every day. If we had taken the time to experience this step, I believe we would've learned many of the basic steps we missed and probably would have given more consideration to whether this business model was the right fit for our profile.

Again, I don't want to discourage you in any way if you believe the restaurant business is for you, but my personal advice for any start up is to work in the type of business you're interested in (possibly part-time), to see what the work flow feels like, even from an employee point of view. You may not be able to see the business financials, but you can learn about the operations of that type of business. I would've been looking at the customer traffic flow; what marketing strategies brought customers in; what the customer complaints were; how management managed; what employees thought about the company; how problems were solved; how I felt working the hours of operation and how managers and supervisors answered probing questions, etc. There is a lot you can learn in this step.

If we had worked in this business, at least part-time, we may have realized the following: how hard it really is to find good, reliable help (which could mean you can never really pull away from the business), that the profit margins can be very small and that we weren't as passionate about the restaurant business model so much as the idea of owning a physical business with automatic traffic.

For those of you who are thinking of going into this business model, or are already in it, it could be the perfect match for your skills, background and personality. Conducting the proper research and taking the basic steps I've provided here would've revealed this to us.

There was one guy, who owned a drive-thru fast food restaurant in front of our business, and we noticed he was always on-site, but he loved it and didn't seem to mind the years it may take for him to gain freedom from being an on-site owner. He told us his margins were also small and growing slowly, but that he loved what he did every day and that's what made the difference.

For us, it felt like we had replaced a job with a job. We had not been realistic in matching our profile to the type of business model we were investing in. We've since successfully discovered the correct business model for us, but the lessons learned have been bitter-sweet.

In my experience and lessons learned, the step in this chapter should be taken before you invest money into any business venture. It is a part of your research that could be done as you are saving your startup money—and it costs nothing to try it.

CHAPTER 8

Don't be afraid to spend the money to hire "your team" (attorney, CPA, Realtor, Tax Advisor, Mentor etc.)

The lesson learned here is pretty simple, but hard to do when you're looking on the surface and not at the big picture. In your mind, you may think you're saving money. You tend to *skimp* on these services, but they are not the items in your budget to *skimp* on. You think that these are tasks you can do yourself to save money and there are such tasks, but these are not those. We regret not having our own professional team to represent us in all aspects.

Don't be afraid to spend the money to hire *your team* (attorney, CPA, realtor, tax advisor, financial counselor or mentor, etc.) to represent you and look out for your best interests. For example, we should've had an attorney to evaluate and advise us on all of the contracts, before we signed them, including the franchise agreement, the building lease contract, the construction build-out contracts, etc. We tried to save money by allowing the franchise representative and ourselves to review our contracts – BIG MISTAKE!

At the end of the day, this particular franchise was looking out for their best interest – to sell a franchise (not all are like this). The realtor worked for the owner of the building we leased and was looking out for the owner's best interest. The construction contractors were independent and, of course, were looking out for their best interests.

Everyone will say that they are trying to provide you with the best service, and they pretend to be looking out for your interests also, but when things go wrong, you're left alone to figure out how to clean up the mess. Hiring your professional team helps you to keep those messes to a minimum and help to clean them up when they do happen. Remember, this was a new business model for us; we had never operated in this type of business industry. We knew computer-telecom engineering and other home-based business concepts, not lease contract negotiation or construction contract negotiations. In essence, we had switched fish tanks and were swimming with sharks instead of fish and not even realizing it. Danger, danger!

Here are a few examples of what went wrong for us because we did not hire our professional team: 1. Several maintenance problems occurred in our leased space, as we operated our restaurant, which we thought the landlord should take care of but he would not and had the lease to support him.

By the way, if I had it to do over, I would prefer to buy a stand-alone building. Or, I would have the landlord build out the basic inside shell including the dry walls, plumbing, electrical, concrete, and as many other needed things as possible. At one point, rainwater was leaking into the front window and door of our restaurant and the landlord didn't want to repair it. Of course, he attempted to place the expense on us. We hired an attorney to threaten him; he then had the repairs made. The grease trap was shared by everyone in the shopping center and when it would get clogged, the landlord would not help and the city would shut us down until it was repaired. This problem continued more often than anticipated and we always seemed to be the business in the shopping center to pay for the repair expense.

2. In the beginning, the franchise corporate office indicated they had many marketing plans to help market the franchise, which is a big part of why you buy a franchise, but they did not deliver on their promises. We were left to figure out all of our own marketing strategies ourselves.

3. When disagreements arose during the construction build-out, the contract always favored the contractor and not us. For example, the plumber installed all the plumbing and, before the restaurant even opened, they realized the piping was installed incorrectly and was going to cause future problems. The plumber didn't want to correct his mistake because it would mean cutting through the concrete, which was going to be expensive. You guessed it, they wanted us to pay for this expense, and we knew that it was not right, but the contract was in their favor. With input from our general contractor, the plumber did make the repairs at his expense. Small claims court would have cost us more money we didn't have.

4. Finally, our bookkeeping and taxes became a daunting task. I wish we had hired a bookkeeper. We performed the task of daily bookkeeping and hired a CPA to do our quarterly taxes. Using a CPA was a good choice because our CPA saved us money through tax write-off rules we had never even heard

of. You could also have the CPA review your initial financial business reports and your financial estimates. They do taxes for many other small businesses also, and could give you good input. A CPA and tax adviser study and stay abreast of all the many tax laws and changes and can save you thousands of dollars. Even though you may pay hundreds for their service, you save thousands and still come out ahead. Keep the big picture in mind.

If you don't spend the up-front cost for these professional services, it may seem like you're saving money but, on the back-end or over the long term, you are losing. Remember, the object of the game is to win. You need these players on your team; this is an important rule of the game.

CHAPTER 9

Good help is hard to find

I'm sure you've heard this before. When we look back on all of our lessons learned, this is one of the most difficult, yet it holds most of the humor, and we still laugh at some of the employee issues that arose. We must have had the craziest employees out there (sometimes literally). If you don't prepare yourself for this one, it'll make you laugh and cry at the same time—you'll think you're going crazy too!

As the old saying goes, "Good help is hard to find. Everyone wants a job, but no one wants to work!" Finding an employee with good work ethics is difficult, so be prepared for not having your ideal employees, without a good hiring process. The key is a thorough screening process, which is challenging to balance when time is of the essence. In the fast-food industry, employee turn-over can happen really quickly. Our screening process improved over time but, again, there was a learning curve. This was one of the most frustrating tasks for us and was a constant struggle.

We tried to have a professional, but family feel, environment. Most of our candidates were young—from high school age to late twenties—and many were new to the workforce. We figured out that the good ones were there a short time, while on their way to college or other employment with much higher pay. A start-up business has a limited pay structure, but even more limited is the time to replace and train a new employee who can be efficient. By the time we figured out the key to the hiring process, it was late in the game (we had also figured out this business model was not a good fit for our profile). We had, on average, 15 - 25 employees on staff, mostly part-time, and 1 full time manager (sometimes more, sometimes less).

If I could yell SCREENING PROCESS, that's what I'm doing, right now! We really didn't know much about hiring in this environment. We thought, "How hard can it be when the corporate franchise gives you a process, right?" That corporate process was so general, that it could have gone in the trash. First, the fast food — or quick service — business has a high turnover rate, but there's still a learning curve for hiring and keeping good employees. It seemed we opened our business so fast and did our hiring just as fast.

We had a standard application form, from the office supply store; created additional interview questions to add to what the franchise provided; interviewed potential employee's once; called references (most of which we could not reach); briefly discussed the interview results with management (my husband and the one manager we had)—then we made a decision, usually within a couple of days. So how did we get so many crazy, incompetent employees? Simple, we didn't have a detailed screening process, really didn't know what to look for and always seemed to be rushing to hire. Time was of the essence. I don't have the perfect solution to this problem, but we did learn a few things that I will share with you.

Before I tell you the lessons learned, I must tell you about a few of our employees. Our first employee watched as our restaurant's space was in construction. He came to the construction site often and was so excited about the possible job opportunity. He lived within walking distance, we interviewed him and he showed a lot of enthusiasm about the opportunity. After the restaurant was finally open and we started to train him, we noticed that he was not catching on at all, even with the simple tasks. We also started noticing his off the wall comments and actions. He seemed to be intelligent in the interview and showed so much excitement, we just knew this was a good match. After a couple of weeks of trying to train – once we realized that it was not going to work – he admitted that he had lied about much of what was indicated on his resume, including education and work history, admitted he had mental challenges and was on medication (which he was not taking properly). We had suspected this after working with him for a couple of days, but how did we miss this in our interview? Simple, we were rushing and did not have a thorough hiring process.

We had several more misses of this kind, but started to recognize the signs sooner. We also had a couple of thieves, a person who was wanted by the Federal Government (drug sales related; it blew our minds), a borderline sexual misconduct incident, a few liars and many lazy employees. One of our thieves would steal food and we caught him on camera, reported it to the police and fired him.

Another one was a little slicker and, as she was on the register, she would slip $20 dollar bills in her pocket. We could never catch her doing it, so we created a new procedure of being accountable for your cash drawer (register) when you take possession and when you close out the register for your shift. If your drawer came up short, that amount would be taken out of your pay check. All of a sudden, the money stopped coming up missing! She ended up quitting soon after this new rule was put in place. I see how these people can slip through the cracks and many companies hire them not realizing what they're really getting.

We also had very good employees that we rewarded with positive feedback and, sometimes, money incentives. We had a few employees who worked really hard, were efficient and honest; it was a pleasure working with them. By the end of our restaurant venture, we actually had improved a lot on our hiring process and were choosing good employees. The business was starting to have a family feel with proficient workers.

My message is only to tell you to take the required time to set up a thorough hiring process that has been proven to work (using best practices), spend the required time to create a thorough screening process and try not to make a decision too quickly, even when you feel the pressure to hire people fast. This is when you end up hiring CRAZY!

We had situations where up to 5 employees left within the same week, all for different reasons. In one instance, one left to go back to school, another found a better paying job, another moved, another was let go due to misbehaving, and the other quit because of playing sports in school! Almost a third of our staff quit in one week and we felt the pressure to hire more employees quickly, so that our business and service was not affected. Many companies struggle with this balance, but you need to find out what successful companies in your industry are doing and use their hiring practices. Again, this is called using *best practices*, described on Wikipedia as *using the method or technique that is consistently showing superior results*.

CHAPTER 10

Understand your short term and long term growth

You should have a good idea what your growth will look like in 3-5-10 years. This information is usually detailed in your business plan. In our business plan, we also included our growth projection on how we would grow our first location and additional locations, but didn't understand, realistically, how small the restaurant profit margins can be with one or two restaurants. Yes, we knew we wanted to grow and own at least three or four locations, but we didn't realize we needed three or four locations to see the profits needed to sustain our current lifestyle.

With only one location, the business could only afford to sustain itself, which meant we either needed more restaurant locations—fast—or we had to get additional jobs to pay our household bills. Opening a new location would've required up-front money we didn't have, at the beginning stage of our business and, each time we attempted to pull ourselves out of the business, our management could not sustain the business operations successfully, so we were stuck. As mentioned in previous chapters, this made us re-evaluate our decision on the business model we chose; we felt it was not a good situation and ended up closing our doors.

The lesson learned here is: you cannot create a business plan that plays into your ideal view of success. You must do sufficient research and take a hard, realistic look at how you will grow your business. This includes interviewing other business owners in your industry who have a proven success record and who will be transparent with you. Don't be afraid to ask—because they will be able to give you realistic projections—and don't find yourself being overly optimistic to the point of non-realistic.

CHAPTER 11

Know when to hold or fold and move on

I'll never forget a statement made by one of the mentors we had during our early research of the restaurant business. I guess I could call him a mentor because he did share a few tips with us, though not real transparent numbers. This mentor owned a couple of restaurants, at the time, and we noticed that he worked very hard, long hours and had grown knowledgeable of the food industry.

One day, as he was sitting with us and giving us some advice and information about operating in the food industry business, he said, "Be careful you don't get caught up in a situation where you are chasing fool's gold." I remember thinking how off the wall that comment was at the time. I don't remember him expanding on the comment, but I remembered the comment and the weirdness of it. As we were all excited, with money in hand, ready to open our restaurant business, we didn't ask him to elaborate. What he said went in one ear and out the other, very quickly.

My husband and I never mentioned how weird that comment felt until we were knee- deep into operating our own restaurant business. BAM!! It hit us; we suddenly understood what he meant. We were each working about 80+ hours a week (7 days a week), making almost $500K annually (gross) from the business, but only netting less than 25K a year for our profit. My husband's salary was about 5 times that amount when he worked in corporate (working only 40 hours a week). So the $500K looked like a good amount of money but, after all the expenses and all the long, hard hours worked, we were only left with less than 25K.

In other words, the profit margins were so small that we would need at least four of these restaurants to even get close to the kind of money our household bills required (not including my salary). We were chasing *Fools Gold*! Uhggg... What looked like a fun business for us was not, and what looked like a lot of money for us was not. Of course, many entrepreneurs thrive in this business industry and environment and you might be one of those who will do great, but do your due diligence.

We are not alone in our experience as small business owners. The survival rate for new businesses, given by the U.S. Dept. of Commerce, Bureau of Labor Statistics, is 7 out of 10 new businesses survive at least 2 years, 5 out of 10 survive at least 5 years, a third survive at least 10 years and a quarter stay in business 15 years or more. Which reminds you of the saying that, "if it was easy, everyone would be doing it."

When you get as far as we had gotten in a major business project (major to our budget) and you have invested so much of your time and money, it's hard to know when it's time to pack up and move on. There were many reasons why this business was not working for us. So, we made a decision that if we did not feel differently about the business by our deadline, we'd sell or close our doors. Selling was not a good option since the profits were so small and the risk factors were so large, so closing was our only other option.

Closing our business was a difficult and emotional decision. You think about all the money, time, tears and sweat invested and how it will affect others involved, such as family investors and employees, but, when it came down to it, we didn't want to be a deer in headlights either. The fact is, as entrepreneurs, we have to make difficult decisions every day — and this was the most difficult.

Realistically, looking at the numbers, we could not afford to continue going deeper into debt, due to our personal household bills not being met, and we were not enjoying the work either. You can't be blinded by optimism and ignore the facts. You also shouldn't focus on, but do consider, the worst case scenario for your business and how you will handle it.

In the beginning, when making your business plan, you will also need to determine what options you have for your exit strategy. You plan how to operate and grow the business, but how would you wind down the business, if you had to? What if you couldn't sell it? This should be planned on the front end and not the back end, just like investing in real estate.

For an entrepreneur, owning a business provides many challenges and opportunities for learning, so I do believe the risks are worth trying and can be very rewarding. In the case that it fails, sometimes bigger and better opportunities are in store for you that will cause you to gain more than you've lost. After we closed this business, we went through a rough time before we found the right business model that fit our profile. Now that we've found the right business model and have grown so much wiser, we appreciate our experiences. We've taken our experiences, knowledge, research and those hard lessons learned, and we now use them to benefit others — in turn, benefiting ourselves.

Our current businesses include an internet marketing company, with profitable retail stores and websites online; I am a published author of non-fiction books that not only inspire others, but also solve problems for a niche group; and my husband has his own retail websites and is consulting as a project manager. All of the work we do now allows us to work from home, set up businesses on autopilot (internet), flexibility in our schedule to accept more money making opportunities, flexibility to travel more, spend more time watching our son grow and we now make more money than we've ever made, which are all on our list of "what we love to do" (See Chapter 2).

By operating these businesses and working from home, we have the flexibility to continue acquiring additional business opportunities that add to our wealth-building goal of millionaire status. We have focused our efforts on the concept of *passive income,* using the multiple streams of income strategy. Wikipedia defines *passive income* as income from real estate investments, a business owners' system that is on autopilot, or royalties from patents for your intellectual property (such as books, songs, etc.).

Our current business model not only allows us to work

remotely from home, or anywhere in the world, our workers are all virtual assistants, not requiring the normal payroll or HR attention. Only through my past experiences have I discovered what I truly enjoy and what I'm good at. Some people never figure out their passion, so I'm very thankful to be able to do the work I love and for my new found successes.

CHAPTER 12

A Final Note

If you can't visualize yourself following these 10 basic concepts, then you have not completed enough research and/or you need to think long and hard about whether the business model you're pursuing is for you. I know for sure that if we had taken the time and effort to complete these 10 important steps, we would've realized that the restaurant's business model wasn't for us. Not that I don't appreciate the learning experience, but I believe that understanding these concepts before I invested thousands of dollars would have allowed for better decisions that would've saved a lot of money and time.

You are going to make your own business venture mistakes and I believe that mistakes are steps toward wisdom. But, I do believe that there are a few basic rules, or a basic blueprint, that can alleviate making too many start-up mistakes. A few can be alleviated through research, knowledge gained and the wisdom of others. Learn from your mistakes and the mistakes of others. This is why we have higher learning institutions with teachers, professors, mentors and books with information, rules and blueprints to follow.

Look out for my next series of books on *how to start making money on the internet* and *how to publish your first book.*

To Your Success!

If you are interested in more small business information, inspiration, free useful forms and much more, visit my blog at www.mymultimoneystreams.com

ABOUT THE AUTHOR

Mia Haley is an experienced Entrepreneur, Author, Blogger, Investor and Educator. She enjoys writing books about her favorite subjects and sharing her stories, experiences and research to inspire new and aspiring entrepreneurs and wealth builders. She currently spends her time writing books and operating her online Internet Marketing business, including affiliate marketing, retail websites and maintains her personal blog at www.mymultimoneystreams.com.

Mia is a dream chaser and is in constant pursuit of a purpose driven life; along the way, she is encouraging others to find their purpose also. Her style of writing is a combination of education through research, step by step programs to solve a niche problem and inspirational storytelling through lessons learned. Through this combination, she's able to teach others how to solve a problem and be entertained as they learn.

Although she used her B.A. degree in Communications for the corporate environment, she chose to leave her successful corporate career and pursue entrepreneurial dreams, which provides limitless business opportunities, growth and successes. She now enjoys the work she does daily as a consultant for individuals and corporations, and as an entrepreneur. She enjoys sharing what she learns along the way. During her spare time, she enjoys reading, writing, traveling and spending precious time with her loving husband, son, extended family and friends who've always been supportive and encouraging of her many ventures: the good ventures, the bad ones and the ugly ones.

www.ingramcontent.com/pod-product-compliance
Lightning Source LLC
Chambersburg PA
CBHW050540210326
41520CB00012B/2652